The Formality of the Page

Tobias Roberts

THE FORMALITY
OF THE PAGE

AND OTHER POEMS

DALKEY ARCHIVE PRESS

Library of Congress Cataloging-in-Publication Data
Names: Roberts, Tobias, 1953- author.
Title: The formality of the page : and other poems / Tobias Roberts.
Description: First Dalkey Archive edition. | Victoria, TX : Dalkey
Archive Press, 2018.
Identifiers: LCCN 2017035397 | ISBN 9781628971859 (softcover :
acid-free paper)
Classification: LCC PS3618.O316453 A6 2017 | DDC 811/.6--dc23
LC record available at https://lccn.loc.gov/2017035397

www.dalkeyarchive.com
Victoria, TX / McLean, IL / Dublin

Dalkey Archive Press publications are, in part, made possible through
the support of the University of Houston-Victoria and its programs in
creative writing, publishing, and translation.

Printed on permanent/durable acid-free paper.

Acknowledgments

This book would not have been possible without the advice, editorial suggestions, and collaboration of my friend and editor, Jacob Miller, a colleague generous in his efforts and time spent with me in this poetic endeavor.

For Rebecca,
the light that never fails

&

For Jacob,
my friend, mentor, editor, and colleague

Contents

The Formality of the Page

Racing Thoughts

I can't understand exactly what they're saying;
And yet, I know they're trying to pin me
Down. The syllables that pass without seeing
The webs that are woven out of mental debris.

It's a fact, they act like I'm not here;
But what are they? And even if they're mine,
They mock and disobey me. At once, near
And far, how am I to guess what they mean?

A target for ridicule as a boy, I was teased
By those who had less noise in their heads,
Until I'd crawl off like a spider, diseased,
With my mind spinning a thousand threads.

Perhaps for others, thoughts are also weaving
Sometimes, yet they eventually settle down.
But me—I'm still jumpy, even now, waving
At shadows, and my head's rarely my own.

Fleeting Glance

I took her smile home with me tonight
After she walked past me on the street,
Talking on her cell phone. She did not
See me, but I caught her smile in the net
Of my gaze and nestled to it straight
Away. Now, I'm alone and uncertain,
As her lips flutter then rest on the curtain.

On the Ugliness of Other Lives

Usually, I don't like talking to anyone,
Except my garbageman, who understands
More, I think, than so many. His hands
Move steadily as he picks up the rubbish
And he speaks words no one will publish,
Though they should. I help him carry some

Trash to the truck, and when we're together,
I feel connected to him, how he can hum
As he carries the crap the world leaves him.
Beyond his job, I only know he lives alone,
But feel we've both seen more than any line
In my poems can say. My poems will gather

Dust and be dumped into Time's fog and mist.
With him, I grasp the ugliness of other lives,
As well as my own—the hefty bags full of lies,
The broken bric-a-brac and ruin that gets tossed,
All the wreckage accumulated and left to be lost—
And I see the garbageman's work is truer than most.

Half-Light

for Peter Roberts (1949-1987)

In this light they won't see the small,
Pale scars on the inside of my wrist.
Let them watch me. I'll stand tall
Inside the door. I don't need a rest.

I'll forget I'm on a dimly lit stage,
Forget the worry scraping my skull
Of how my wife and kids will gauge
My act as they get ready for school?

Here, there's no need to shudder.
They won't see my hands tremble,
Or the way I look over my shoulder.
In this half-light there's no trouble.

A Brother's Remains
for Peter Roberts (1949-1987)

In the end, pressing the cold barrel close
And teasing the trigger with his finger
Must've felt more like poetry than prose,
With a scrimmage of insight you'd figure

Was the product of excessive reflection—
But there was no note, only old clothes,
Jeans and a sweater, to hint at the direction
Of his thoughts or suggest why he chose

To do it. Still, I wondered if he meant to warn
Me? The jeans were torn, just as he was.
His sweater with the hole in it, was also worn
Out. But now I see a man sometimes does

What he does, with no rhyme, rushing to sever
All ties, until that rush blurs into forever.

My Head Is Also in Clouds

In the rain, thoughts of my brother pour

Down what's obvious from the sky:

He's washed away, gone—can say no more.

What did I do wrong? What didn't I try?

What might I have said to Peter to clarify

My head is also in clouds that swarm,

That I too have my place in the storm.

Oubliette

—*There is nothing covered, that shall not be revealed; and hid, that shall not be known.*
Matthew: 10:26

Here, where the black depth is filled
With our hushed secret, in silence, we're led
To forget the family crest. All has failed—
All in our home, me as well—All have lied.
There is a dark stain here, as we wish air
And hearts were less cold. Across the floor,
We hesitate to step, tread so lightly, whisper
Of Peter, now dust, and look at the door.

But then I see my brother enter—his hair
Wet, skin dripping, as he starts to climb
Out of the pit, explaining to our father:
Even when it seemed I'd get no further,
I knew I'd find my way back to claim
My rightful place as your son, your heir.

Elegy for Hart Crane

"Crane had been in the sailors' quarters the previous night, trying to make one of the men, and had been badly beaten. Just before noon, a number of us were gathered on deck . . . Just then we saw Crane . . . in pajamas and top-coat; he had a black eye and looked generally battered. He walked to the railing, took off his coat, folded it neatly over the railing (not dropping it on deck) . . . Then, suddenly, he vaulted over the railing and jumped into the sea."
--From an eyewitness to the events at sea in 1932.

Having wooed the wrong sailor,

Drunk and dropping into the sea,

No port in sight, bruised in salt and green,

Certain in his flesh and bones he was a failure,

He thrashed in the waves of a wounded night

So we wouldn't have to. Hear the voice

Contained in a mind inclined toward vice

And romantic excursions that came to naught.

Hear the voice tangled in the seaweed of doubt,

With images tied tight as any sailor's knot.

Today, his verses still swim though he cannot,

And though he died broke, it is we who are in debt.

Unapologetic, he leaped into the sea,

Back to mother depths, with so much left to say.

Sestets on a Train

The subway we're on hurtles along
As her trembling fingers rise to her face.
In the crowd, she stands out alone—
The rest of us are all actors in a farce.
Center stage, she covers her eyes
And, with her chest heaving, starts to cry.

Others look away as her fingers move
To her mouth and tug at her lips.
At the next station, with nothing to prove,
Brittle as glass, she starts to collapse—
Or should I say, shatter? She appears stoned,
Her head bobs and, muddled as I am, I understand.

Watching the Sunset

Today, at dusk, with her cancer grown so hopeless,
I sat by mother's hospital bed with a cup of tea,
Watching the room filling up with her grief and loss
Till there was no space for me, who she didn't see.

Out the window, as the sun was sinking to mist,
She whispered to herself, "I see it, how all's folly,
How at birth we're marked for death, wholly
Fated to end in the midst of all that's unmissed."

I said, "No, you're wrong—you'll be missed by me."
But she didn't hear me and as the sun sank so did she.

Six Feet Down

Out of the crooked timber of humanity,
no straight thing was ever made.
--Immanuel Kant, 1784

When I'm angled into dirt, like a slant rhyme,

And the polished brass on my coffin, my box,

Has rusted, and there are no more great books

For me to read, and maybe no soul left to roam . . .

Then, though the lacquered wood on my coffin

Contains the grain of words, sanded and said,

What'll come of what went unwritten, unread,

But remains in the timber knots I felt so often?

Is it possible on some mourner it will dawn,

What's buried, though hidden six feet down?

Achilles in His Tent

'Dost thou wish to fight? To kill? To see rivers
of blood? Great heaps of gold? Herds of captive
women? Slaves? And other, still other spoils?
...*Dost thou wish to love divinely?*
--*Gabriele D'Annunzio*

I see it all: the burning of the Greek ships,

Patroclus's death, my flawed efforts to try

Reason with Fate and the detached shits

Perched on Olympus, sitting on high.

Zeus means for me, my friends and foes

To all die for his precious amusement,

But here, in my tent, I can still shake a fist

At the gods, without needing a monument.

Screw Agamemnon—screw my own death!

Now, I'll just stay put to digest the theft

Of Patroclus from me and, with my last breath,

Consider what I failed to say before he left.

    It matters little if or how a so-called hero dies;

    History will decide my story, including the lies.

Carefully Try Balance

1.

Within winter's windy lexicon, where
Is the word to explain his freezing eyes?
Tonight, in a howling blizzard, he wears
An odd blue smile that chills me like ice.

His face shifts between weak and strong,
But either way, coldness stubbles his cheek.
As I write, I shiver, suffering from the sting
Of his silent waiting, daring me to speak.

Tired of language's false ambition—the old
Game where thoughts and words can match—
I endure his silence as I endure the cold,
Biting my lip, without understanding much.

    This song's business was to be its reach,
    But its grasp only finds me afraid of speech.

2.

As I walk away from him, I'm locked in snow.
Let covered streets tell, what day, what night
Began dissolving into the blizzard-bound now.
Here, I am pelted by icy pebbles that do not
Stop coming from the gauze above, falling,
Like his coldness—and I recognize the feeling.

As I touch the snow with my blue fingers,
It melts to tears. Icicles also cry for me, for
My life. I shiver and consider what lingers—
As a girl, my mother's voice brought fear.
As a young woman, on a wharf, I saw a man
Who smiled at me, but I did not understand.

That's what's left in the snow's blanket—
A girl's fear, a woman's longing—what most
Endures is chiseled to something I blink at
As I'm numbed into my own gray ghost—
A glimpse of a mother's knees, a man's smile,
Boats tacking in the harbor, an urge to be wild.

3.

Back home, I carefully weigh the fierce
Coldness of our moments in dawn's light,
To see which side the raised scale prefers,
Leaning, as it must, to the left or right.

I won't wake him as the ice clings to leaves;
I'll wait for the fury to come from the sun—
Me, I am the branch that, breathing, lives.
Me, I am the silence waiting for a sound.

Carefully alone, rock forward and back,
Feel the dirt and dust, rise up, slide down,
Then level a glance through the black
Soot and white snow glazing the dawn.

Carefully consider, perhaps no balance
Weighs or illuminates all by a mystic sun,
But still try. Though life and romance
Can be cruel, both are over too soon.

Waiting

I have yet to hear an angel call to me.
In silence, the sky is a faded blue house.
Clouds are white, unwashed, tattered sheets
And the sun runs away to no one's surprise.
Elm trees have poorly colored greenish leaves
And stand outside because someone said they must.

This dull and much copied street believes
In dark macadam, cracked edges, dirt and dust.
Light comes from wherever light comes:
That is the end of knowledge at night.
No voice is heard; there are just crumbs,
Crumpled paper, empty bottles in the street.

Ivan Ilyich Dying

*Just then Ivan Ilyich fell through, saw light, and it was
revealed to him that his life had not been what it ought . . .*
--Leo Tolstoy, 1886

The house is taken apart brick by brick

By swift, rustling hands as light fades away

While the owner, on morphine, nods in the back,

Forgetful of the last debt he's yet to repay.

But it isn't a sum of money he owes,

Instead it's the gestures left unreturned:

The unreturned smiles from those he knows,

As he wrestles with all he hasn't learned.

He fights, unwilling to accept this as his last day;

And as his arms flail about, he hits his son's head.

Now he sees how the boy's holding his hand, how

He's kissing it, and whispers, "Take him away now."

Finally, he tries to say *Forgive me*, but instead

Says, "Forgo." Then he sees: he has no need to stay.

Henry Darger Searching Trash

Henry Darger, a reclusive janitor in Chicago,
wrote a 15,000-page novel only discovered
by his landlord after Darger's death in 1973.

With only dry-throated grunting left of his Voice,

He prays, pen pressed in earth's vise, for the Word.

In the alley, the spray-painted message reads:

"Get Head—Call Vivien—$40—" Next to it,

He scrawls: "Yes, need new head, own's unfit.

Is new mind included too?" He's certain he bleeds

Ink, huddled and huddling in cast-off coat, wired,

Hyena-laugh-turned-cackle fighting city noise—

Like a metal trash can, he's rusted by life's demands.

He watches his breath steam a ghostly loaf of bread.

Perhaps Vivien's a petite, pink-cheeked child,

Innocent, thin-limbed, in danger? Here, chilled

In a slate-gray downpour, counting out each breath,

Henry paces, wrestling his rain-drenched demons.

A Neighbor's Note

The quiet man who wrote this note is dead;
Here is where black ink sank into white paper.
Perhaps he was teased by a voice in his head
And sick of being broke, living like a pauper.

Study the evidence left behind: dribbles
Of ink scrawled as if he did not even think
His note would be read, so illegible, scribbles
Too frenzied to tell what took him to the brink.

It makes no sense: the note or his death—
But isn't this so often ink on a page's plight?
What's certain? This note can't draw a breath,

Like the quiet man, now buried in his plot.

Green Eyes

In the dim light, when I kiss you, your mouth
Opens, without asking what is or is not real,
Even as our hands tremble and travel south.

Perhaps I'm pretending we both still feel
That we're one touch, one lust, without lies—
So what if my imaginings leave me a fool?

It seems, no matter how much one tries,
No one finds an ideal us. But I still wish
I knew what's behind your cold, green eyes.

Night Again

Night again, and I'm looking for words to define
The undefinable, while all you want to do is sleep.
So instead of bothering you, I lift my pen to find,
Or try find, in verse some clarity that won't slip
Away from me. But isn't clarity always so slight
It can fly away at a touch, just as I fear you'll leave .
Me eventually, despite this frail thing we call love?

Excursions into Philosophy

(after Edward Hopper)

I tried, really tried to tell her what I meant.

But it did no good—I was clumsy, of course—

It ended with me in the wrong, scrimmage-spent.

And yet now—what's left but the worst curse?

She's sidelined on the bed, her back to me, as if fate

Keeps her faking sleep, while I can't dare caress

Her or speak. This move is her checkmate

In our marital game of chess. I want to scream

The worst scream, but she's rendered me mute.

Mostly, I guess she just wants me to scram,

Just hit the road and leave her alone, but it seems

Madness holds me here, thinking "goddamn."

I am

You write down on paper the words *I am*—
But what good comes of three letters alone?
It's just the start of what will end in a line
Of words like, *not in love,* after the iamb.

Wouldn't it be better spoken than written,
Free to blend with barking dogs, roaring cars—
Better said aloud than kept with your secret cares
On a page? I know, lately, we've been rotten

Together. So say it, don't jot it down
In your unlocked journal for me to find.
Let your voice utter what's on your mind,
Whisper if you wish. I don't give a damn.

The Rustling of Sheets

For unseen worlds, her feet feel. A sigh
Escapes her lips as her body revels,
Though her panting passion can't defy
What her solitude as I'm pushing reveals.
Still, this is how the white nova bursts,
Where the engulfing, embracing flame
Finds her squeezing her own breasts
And, for a moment, forgetting my name.
But, after letting go of one final groan,
She's done, rolls over in the bed, and lies
On the other side. The flash of light gone,
Without any thought, she closes her eyes.
      But I, awake, hear the rustling of sheets
      And the way the pillow whispers of defeats.

Dagger Moon

Damocles, a flatterer, pronounced
Dionysius I, the ruler of Syracuse,
The Happiest of men, whereupon
Dionysius, inviting him to experience the
Happiness of a monarch, placed him at
A banquet where a naked sword hung over
His head suspended by a single hair.

Thinking of a knife's sideways smile

Makes me think of this wife of mine.

After sex, she's close, sleeping, still

Tangled in rustling sheets, as a moan

Escapes from her and the moon, a blade

Of silver, is suspended above my head

By a hair. Is it the hour for spilled blood,

For the sword to descend, unravel thread?

Do they truly sleep, I wonder, the moon

And my wife now, or are they pretending,

Plotting to do me in behind the silver mien,

The closed eyes, twisting and descending?

Should I stay in bed, if they are indeed

Plotting, or move, rather than end up dead?

High Wire

I can't say why your leaving put me on a wire
With no net below, blinking and wondering where
My steps across this shivering line might lead.
Even now, your last words in my head grow loud.

I admit it—I don't know if our love was real;
Perhaps you don't know either or don't care.
As it is, you've left me on a high wire, in the role
Of a dizzy acrobat, legs wobbling, with no cure

For my being unbalanced. If I fall, if you glance
At my descent, I suppose you'll again curse
Your same last words to me, "Fuck romance"—
As you did when you left our marriage's circus.

Fear the Clown

After I'm down from the high wire, on the ground,
Fear, the angry clown, lips painted red into a sneer,
Is at my side, mocking me, waving with false grand
Gesticulations. Circus spinning, I look for you, stare,
Until the bearded lady leers my way, then I frown,
Sick when I think her wink is for me, not the clown.

As I walk, toe-to-toe, Fear mimics my steps beside
Me, matching my stride, wildly aping my gestures.
Stumbling in the tent, it seems, I've no way to hide—
Not even for a moment can I dodge the gaudy jester.
I don't know why he's here, scratching his red nose
When I sneeze or kick the sawdust floor with my toes.

Even now, I still hear the demonic clown's threat
Snarled in curses, muttered in my ear between shows,
Making clear his plan as I watch him light a cigarette.
He plans to have me wearing his oversized shoes,
To see my lips twisting into his sneer with despair,
To see me doing pratfalls, clouds of dust everywhere.

Parting Gift

At first light, I wake up, stretch, and groan,
Then, with my eyes squinting, I am stunned
To see my Muse smiling as she places a gun
And one shining bullet on the nightstand.
Frozen, I pretend to be still sleeping till
I hear her leave my bedroom. Then I lift
Myself up, start pacing, and finally tell
Myself, in her shoes, I also would've left.

I still smell her scent and recall our love,
But realize she, as a Goddess, could discern
My thoughts so well she would leave
Such a parting gift for the end I yearn.
And now alone, the only voice I can hear
Comes from the gun whispering in my ear.

A Poet's Lament

Each breath I take is short and less
Alive. My Voice chokes shredded ice.
What's recalled of us, it seems, is loss
And worn-away words without your face.

After you left, before I could blink—
Door closed, pistol pawed, curses
Muttered—I was again facing a blank
Page alone, scribbling shabby verses.

But I'll erase my words, each letter
Fails to explain love or the need to write
About what I don't understand. In litter,
Crumpled pages cover the floor. Tonight,

    None of my words cohere. I'm a wretch
    And clarity, like you, is beyond my reach.

In Your Dark Eyes

— scelesta, vae te, quae tibi manet vita?
quis nunc te adibit? cui videberis bella?
...quem basiabis? cui labella mordebis?
--Catullus, Poem 8

Once your lashes blinked at me, I felt no fear

Of a future without you nestling me, always near.

Once, staring into the furnace of your dark eyes,

I was warmed by flames that burned like coal.

But since you left me, I've realized only the ice

Of your last look over your shoulder, the cold,

Remains. And now I see only a frozen line,

A glacier, where your future will be defined.

In that time, no one will hear your drunken rants.

Your face will be dried wrinkles of cracked leather.

Your bloodshot eyes will find no man to glance

Back. Your tears and cries will work you into a lather

When your white hair hits your pillow, and you slip

Off, all alone, after drinking yourself to sleep.

Game Over

The road ends with a line of cement;
Ahead is only midnight and swaying grass.
Headlights glare—what's any of it meant?
Families die, clocks tick, time's a gross
Joke and there's nowhere left to go—
I sit in my car watching my breath mist
By the dashboard's dim glow. I know
The game's been played out and I lost.
The rules say it's time to leave the car
And walk into the dark of the frozen field.
A black breeze whispers, "Why care?
Enough of feelings. Enough of what's felt.
Be free of the game, free of its rules,
Free at last of all of our fucked-up roles."

On Reading the Idea of Order in Key West
(for Wallace Stevens)

His words make night and sea a home
For trembling waves to appear.
Here, the singer, a voice of universe,
Survives as more than mere verses.

At dusk, in Key West, my hotel room,
I hope, is in earshot of her voice.
The sky, meanwhile, turquoise-green, shifts
To black as the sun sits and stretches red.

Inside, I listen for her song to hear,
Word by word, the world taking a shape
Which might tell what a sunset means,
And what secret the shifting colors know.

But, what idea of order can exist when
No singer is heard over the air-conditioner,
And no sky "acutest at its vanishing"
Can be seen through drawn curtains?

If order is glimpsed in the ecstasy of words,
Just as stars still penetrate the hard night in

A feeling, curtains in Key West don't matter.
In this sense, it seems, Ramon was wrong.

It wasn't in Politics, or even Religion—
Both still leave me with a need to merge
With words from the sea and find my place
Within the order of phrases from her song.

Words

What finally reduced the *She* I'd loved

To the *Shh* sound you made as you left?

Sadly, between us, there was no more lust,

And my words on paper most likely won't last.

Even all the angry words we spoke are gone,

Triggered and fired, like bullets from a gun.

Eyes blink and water as I recall your ways,

But no words will ever revive the *us* that was.

By the Pool

Night, stir of stars, a woman sits nearby, her mouth
Open. The moonlit blue settles in the hotel pool's
Water. Glancing near the woman's lips, a moth,
Perhaps drawn to the light of her smile, pales
Against her pink skin. Wings flutter a moment,
As do the woman's eyelashes. Then they are gone—
Both the moth and woman leave. I'd meant
To speak to the woman, not of the heart's song,
But just a friendly word, which can so often turn
A key that opens a door, yet I was mute, too
Frozen to utter a sound. And so now, I'm torn
Up inside again, sitting alone, listening to

> How the water, lapping at the side of the pool,
> Is laughing at the sad longings of a lonely fool.

On Youth and Other Failures

When I was a boy, Erato smiled at me once
With her ruby lips moistened by her tongue.
And when she turned, though I wanted to pounce,
I was confused by love or lust—the song unsung.

Back then, I felt invincible, despite being young,
Despite being awkward, clumsy, fumbling, and slow,
Despite an inability to love myself—yet, I was undone
By my inexperience when face to face with Erato.

Since then, though I've chiseled consonants in flint
And smoothed vowels in foaming surf like a fool,
It seems nothing's worked. And tonight, I fell flat
On my face again when Erato appeared by the pool.

Here, in Key West alone, did I think if the light
Of Erato's smile were to appear, some hotel romance
Would ensue? That despite my white hair, I'd let
Myself go? But no, it's too late and I lost my chance.

Dream Verses from Catullus in Key West

Once, Juventius, you laid with me for hours, late
As night's tender arms embraced his lover, Earth,
And Garda's breeze kissed our naked skin that let
Us still connect. Then, our eyes meeting gave birth—
As your youth entwined to my older age—to a vision
Of our souls joined more profoundly than any tales
Told by would-be poets. Once, the sun's invasion
We longed to postpone, in our passion, the tolls
Of morning bells sounding, forever. But that's past.
Rome calls me to face the blade of Caesar's smile
Now and see Lesbia's black eyes again—a path
That ends dark and dank amid the Tiber's smell.

    Still, since you've left me, when you gaze into other eyes,
    I wonder if you look just for lust or a love that never dies?

Path of Descent

Tonight, after it rained, I saw a poem
In the way a single drop can remain,
Displaying an epic grasp on a leaf's vein.
Like me, after you left, it held on, alone,
A bit, but was also poised, waiting to fall,
To collapse, a raindrop, like me, so frail.

When the drop did give in, leave the leaf,
I considered what might be said of my fate,
Of anyone's final fall. Though I've fought
For insight, despite each desperate belief,
Despite our efforts to hold on or be brave—
The path of descent is too rapid, too brief.

Shoreline

Each day, it seems more sand along the shore
Is drawn into the sea, dragged in the undertow.
A handful of land from here, I'm almost sure,
Is gone with each wave—but what do I know?

I can't honestly say how often I stop to notice
Changes and observe around me each shift.
It's enough that I feel ashamed and wince—
Pondering how mostly I don't notice shit.

Both my mind and the sand go out to sea
While new shorelines appear and old
Ones disappear, but how much can I say
Goes unobserved, as I watch waves unfold?

Sailing after the Light

The lighting of the lamp in the boat came first,
No flashlight, just the cast-iron lamp from below—
I wasn't lost, but following the flame dancing fast
Over the sea, glimmering in shredded yellow.

Later, I turned off the ship-to-shore when a sliver
Of light from the moon splintered the water silver.
Then I drifted for hours, navigating blind,
Fascinated by how the moonlight's blend

Of substance and shadow glided gently on
The surface in slanted lines, while the boat
Was tossed this way and that. And, as one
Line led to another, I couldn't come about.

In a Study in Princeton, New Jersey: 1953
(Albert Einstein looks out his window)

The goal of erecting a pure electromagnetic field theory of matter remains
unattained for the time being, although in principle no objection can be raised
against the possibility of reaching such a goal.
--Albert Einstein (from *Out of My Later Years*)

Tonight, after staring so long at the sky,

I see how all the embroidered stars align

And thread through one great tapestry

Hand-woven and suspended by God alone.

Yet, despite a pattern's precision and clues,

The numbers elude me, even as I stare

At stars and wrestle a theorem with claws

Scratching at how intertwined all energies are.

I know the theorem's there, a will-o-the-wisp,

Teasingly in sight, taunting me as I frown,

But she flits back when I try to grasp

Her or take her and make her my own.

Of course, the theorem flirts each time

When we adjust and locate synergy

In an open hand and our hearts climb

To change a field of intertwined energy.

But tonight, with stars beautiful to see,

It seems so close, I don't want to brood

Or whine, but I long for the proof to be

Real as love, which I need more than bread.

In Solitary

Having moved alone into a run-down home, my mouth
Struggles to find my Voice and the words to be heard—
But why? She's no longer here, it's just me and it's hard.
Collecting my muddled thoughts is like buying a myth
From Joseph Campbell as if it was true today. My rubbish,
The crumpled pages of my poorly spun lines, all a bust,
Now cover the parquet floor of my room. But it's best,
I now see—no one in their right mind will ever publish
My work. Since my poems carpet the parquet, no fussing
Readers will scrutinize my scribbling, or try to see life
In my syllables. So I can quit words, with a kind of relief,
Quit trying to explain the ineffable, which keeps refusing

    To be described in any way resembling precision or say

    Anything that offers more than my thoughts drifting at sea.

Insomnia

First night here, three a.m., counting each breath,
The message scratches my mind without a word,
As I toss and try to resist what's always heard—
That I am one day closer to death.

Screw the meds. Let the demons' speculation
Flood my thoughts. Alone, unease will speak
To me, no matter what. Her absence is a spark,
Firing up disappointment with no consolation.

So how am I to face the dark and start
To close my eyes, start to surrender to sleep?
Where is the pillow from which I might slip
To silence, free of my murmuring heart?

On Rereading Emily Dickinson

Unpacking boxes, I come across her book
Of poems, which troubles me, to see—laid
Out in black and white—the terror invade
Her quiet questions put to God's back:

Why fancy I, as my polite Lover—Death?
Why pray I that Time's Passage—cease?
Why do I confine myself within this tall House
Where my brain is not one with God's breath?

From question to question—I know her
Frailty so well—a childhood with a cold father
Appears, shadows in the house, press further—
Asking, despite the absence of an answer.

Cramped in Candlelight

Alone in my new home, I try to write a note
To you. Wind outside also scribbles tonight,
Curses in an obscure language that I know
Offers me, and you, nothing useful or new.

This house, like me, is falling apart, as a line
Comes to mind: *you'll grow old and die alone.*
Or should I say the end of our affair left the book
Of us unfinished, or simply write—take me back?

Now, a fuse blown, I'm cramped in candlelight,
With no electricity to shed light or offer insight.
Once, if my memory is not flawed, I was loved—
Till I was the latest wreckage you chose to leave.

So, I'll blow out the candle—screw this note anyway!
Whatever I pen comes back to just one word: Why?

Mirror Lake

The surface of the lake behind the house remains smooth,
Blue glass without a ripple, despite the stones I throw.
Looking at the water, it seems my efforts to follow through
Have always failed. Unmoving surfaces marked my youth.

What happened? After the stubble of a beard first appeared
On my pale cheeks, I left home, hoping to create a spark,
But kept striking wet flint for years, unable to leave a mark.
Of course, it's an all-too-common story everyone's heard.

So why keep throwing stones at water that remains still?
Perhaps it's just an old habit of mine at this point.
Others leave finished works behind, in words or paint—
Me, I throw stones to no end, as if I've got time to kill.

Punching a Pillow and Feeling Afraid

Yet again, tonight I'm unable to sleep
As my breath races, tightens my throat.
Choking on my familiar panic, I slip
To the hissing in my head—the *thought*.

Here, out the open window, trees
Nod in a breeze like an accusing face,
And I can hear how, at me, their leaves
Are shaking wildly rustling fists

As cars and sirens scream like the line
In my mind, the *thought*: I am a fraud.
Tangled in damp sheets, I am alone—
Punching a pillow and feeling afraid.

Daemon Muse

Why, my Muse, in this house, do you refuse me a word

That I, who struggled forever to find you, long to know?

Why are you now silent, leaving me pacing and wired?

Once you gave me such gifts as that *"sky sobbing snow"*

Line, leading me to pen lyrics, like an inevitable song,

But here your music's gone. What have I done wrong?

A Judge's Eye in the Snow

Midwinter, after another sleepless night, near home
I find a spot in a field of snow, where exposed knots
Of earth look up through melted snow. Say I'm nuts,
But I can discern this dark circle is staring at me alone.

Is my mind, my soul—all ice—being tried by this eye
Surrounded by snow that's judging me, squinting in mud?
If so, whatever I plead, I guess I'll be found guilty, mad;
So why speak of my gnawing fears? No, I won't testify.

On the Corner of a Bad Thought

This is how an ex-wife waits like a whore,
Strutting on the corner of a bad thought
I try to resist, but cannot ignore.

In dreams, meeting her eyes, I see a threat.
Inside her razored gaze, all else pales.
Her look says she has a high price and that

I should just give up and take more pills.
Mornings, when I pace and kick at the floor,
I'm angry she invaded my dreams, still pulls

At my ear: "You're full of shit." The whore's
Hissing refrain still pushes me to agree—
Her words start and finish each internal war.

Houseguest

Lately, I suspect she's under the floor of each room;

For now, I seem to hear her words—not a bard's,

But a bitch's murmur—rising from the floorboards.

Both night and day, pacing or sleeping, my fears roam

As she insinuates her darkness through my thoughts,

Twisting my already racing head, till I see: alert,

Albeit alone, she won't rest till I'm buried in dirt.

Even here, in my new home, the past extracts a cost.

Here, her consistent cackling urges me to retreat,

Ready myself to accept loss, dwelling in night,

To agree that living or longing for light is for naught

And my life's end cannot be fought without defeat.

    True, I've known no kindness since you left me,

    Still, I'll fight the darkness you'd leave me to see.

A Spider's Fear

Like a spider, leaning over the edge of my desk,

My skinny legs scribble my latest web in a spin

Of measured lines, weaving dawn to dusk,

Without recognition, eyes bulging the span

Of my threads, but I wonder what's my fuss

All about? Maybe in my frenzy, I fear a mishap,

A weak tangle or knot as I stretch each line

That seems to construct little more than a trap.

Or is my fear that I'm the one trapped here, alone,

Dreaming of wings and a flight's interrupted trip?

Behind the House, Beyond the Lake

Tonight in the woods, *it's* telling me, screw

You. I hear *it* in the storm, *its* howls and cries.

My head spins as *it* watches me with crystal eyes.

I'm dazed, waiting for what the menace will do

To me. Patient. I can sense *it* is a patient thing.

Perhaps not a thing of bones and blood,

But *it* is still here, rippling each grass blade—

Or is *it* sharpening a blade, poised to spring

At me? Plan. I know *it* plans. *It's* busy.

What's left? I must brace myself, prepare

For *it*, even as I pretend to deny *it* is here.

Yes, I must stay calm; pretend I'm not dizzy.

Dreading the Dawn

I fear midnight less than dawn.
Each repeating tick of the clock
Murmurs as Time tramples the lawn.

I must avoid the dark lake where my fear's drawn,
Drop by drop, with Time's revolver click.
I fear midnight less than dawn.

In this house, I feel my strength drain
As my thoughts race, forming a fluttering flock
That murmurs to me while Time tramples the lawn.

In this house, I still hear *its* roaring drone
Coming closer like a steam locomotive on track.
I fear midnight less than dawn.

With each sunrise, I near the day I'm done
And *its* hands grip me by my neck,
Murmuring how Time tramples the lawn.

I return to my fear, where *it* lives, first began,
And will not be dispelled by any word or trick.
I fear midnight less than dawn,
Constant murmurs, and Time's trampling lawn.

Staring at the Ceiling

It's a losing proposition: laying on the floor, waiting for sleep.

Sleep, same as her—that bitch—no longer visits me. "Please,"

I say, as I stare at the ceiling, and it's the first word to slip

Past my lips, I suddenly realize, since I moved into this place.

Without anyone else's voice, time holds its breath. How long?

I don't know. But I'm a good listener to silence as I wait,

Deserted, as if the ceiling will speak to me. It's all wrong:

Not sleeping, not talking, watching my beard grow white.

The House as an Hourglass

Tonight, I was in bed as sand began grinding the lens
Through which I see all. It started scratching my door—
The sand creeping in, but I didn't look, didn't dare
Sit up in bed or move the way a curious person leans
Forward. There's no believing in a sweet Mr. Sandman,
I thought, as if humming that old song, without flair,
Might save me as more sand sifted in, over the floor.
I already knew it's useless saying it's just in my mind.
As I lay, beached in my bed, not sure what was meant
By the assault of sand rising by my bed frame, shouts
Started in my chest; but feeling spent between the sheets,
Despite the sand's grit scratching my skin, I was silent.

     Mostly, I blamed my head, like the sand's a mistake
     I made, yet it left me uncertain if I'm ever awake.

The Nocturnal Killer

I hear his panting, see his shadow near my back

When I turn—Is this the one who'll be my guide,

My Virgil, skilled in verse, or is he just a maniac,

A menace in my home, from whom I cannot hide?

Why continue on this path where I am not free?

When the sounds of my steps stop, I feel stuck

And hear his steps also stop. He's playing with me—

A blind man tired of tapping his way with a stick.

It's darkest night on the twisting trail of my life

As I roam from room to room, sensing this shadow

Near me is no mentor, but a killer, fingering a knife.

Yet, if he's both, will he and I be one? Will I know?

     Now, I suddenly find myself shivering in the attic,

     Listening to the steps creak, waiting for his attack.

Interregnum

In this run-down old house, the torch
That's lit, hisses like it's eating straw
And leaves granite walls to lurch
In whispering shadows that stray.

The light crouches, burns to be free.
The light is a broadly sweeping hand.
The light rolls away all dark debris,
And shows me what I now understand:

Darkness can be disrobed—its threats
Hidden in the folds of her black gown
Which wrinkle my racing thoughts—
Ironed out by Light's red-hot dance again.

In simple math: flames plus a windy
Breeze equals growth. Fire has no fear—
So the torch must be flung out the window
To burn dry grass, until all is made clear.

The Fire

Gray ashes drift across my windowpane
As the hissing fire sweeps the grass smack-
Dab below me. Entwined with limbs in pain,
Twisting branches beseech me through smoke.
I stare down at them from my attic room above,
Shaking my head for all that burns, but skip
Thoughts of leaving. Nothing stays alive
Forever, despite a vague hope of escape.

What was I thinking, I wonder, as crackling twigs
I hear through my window and the flames I see
Keep me shifting in my seat, watching twinges
Of sparks leap up, like red eyes, staring at me?
      No matter. I'm too burnt-out as it is
      To respond to the looks of red eyes.

The Shut-in

I'm afraid to go out the door—
I want to be locked in—I can feel
How the acid rain is about to pour
On grass that's razor-sharp, burnt steel—
I don't want to look out my window:
Men with rubber coats, hoses, yellow
Eyes looking up—predators—from below—
Yes, their stares will burn me, I know.

All those I once saw as people are gone—
There are only demons of fire—I must hide.
Before the soot, I sat on grass that was green;
Now, on the ground, only gray steel is seen.
All is drenched black, no day or night outside—
In smoke and sweat, I must be shut-in, alone.

A Hazy Mirror

Labored breathing, opaque reddish tissue, unsure
Of each step, roaming one dim room after another
As a light-deprived, glaring fish-eyed creature,
He bumps into a chair here, slams a table there.
Opening more doors, steps straighten, sinews
Strengthen, guide bare feet and grasping hands
To the desk. Groping chewed pencils, he reviews
Grubby ends of dirty erasures and rubber bands
Until, head jerking through smoke, his glazed
Eyes catch himself in a hazy mirror and he laughs.
"It's almost me," he sputters, then leans, raised
Forehead slamming forward, shattering glass.

    Then, blinking, he mutters when he can see
    His bloody face in the shards, *Now it's me.*

The Psychotic Dr. Schreber to His Physician, Dr. Flechsig, 1894

Daniel Paul Schreber was treated in the psychiatric hospital of Leipzig University by Paul Flechsig. In his Memoirs of My Nervous Illness, *Schreber described the treatment he received there. This case gained notoriety after Freud penned a monograph on Schreber.*

Smile, but I know the secret, how you're threaded

To stars you pretend not to see, that you're wedded

To fevers, frail nerves, while me, I'm the bride

Of God, and, from me, a new earth will be bred.

Go, *Herr Doktor*, scratch your chin or your ass.

You're lost in your own madness, your own lust.

Hell, the way you wait to defile me is bad form—

Kleine Flechsig—you're a base and vile worm!

So wriggle, sir, scribble your notes—me, I know

What's ahead, God will translate me and show

Me stripped of what's male—you pathetic weed.

His light will bathe me white, ready to be wed.

Go ahead, Flechsig, call your strong-armed thugs

And turn to my wife with your temperate hugs.

You know! I'm betrothed to God. And that truth,

Little man, shreds you, you posing mental sleuth.

Fear's Song

Tonight Fear flew down on charcoal wings
And cackled her familiar drawn-out cry,
Without melody, across the gray gauze sky.
Of course, I shouldn't listen to how Fear sings,
But I'm weak. I've heard Fear's tunes
So often, the bitter lyrics about darkness
And dying with a stale breath in the breast,
Yet I'm still addicted to the way she croons.

Bartleby Alone

[Bartleby] never spoke but to answer . . .
that for long periods he would stand looking out,
at his pale window behind the screen, upon the dead brick wall . . .
                              --Herman Melville, 1856

I stare into the darkness; my face is pale, sick,

Growing whiter as though being erased.

The high brick wall, thick and shrouded black,

Has lost all traces of a living red.

Ten feet away is fixed, unchanging night.

To look out is easier than to look in.

This office is my coffin, I, its ghost.

The others here wear the idiot's grin.

From them I get bundles of white paper

Scribbled on with blighted black letters

To be copied onto blanks, but I would prefer

Not to corrupt one white sheet to ink-stained tatters.

Life is an office job in the antechamber to death

Where I prefer to stand still and listen to my breath.

Troubled Rest—A Villanelle

Black thoughts are stagnant, yet never sleep
Beneath the skull's caved ceiling hides my heart
When the worm comes out to creep.

Let waves of swimming feelings leap.
The cave is cold; there's no fire, no hearth—
Black thoughts are stagnant, yet never sleep.

Yet hidden in this cave far down deep
Is a grinning shadow of cackling mirth
When the worm comes out to creep.

The shadow has long-fingered words that slip
Through unlit beliefs to find a berth.
Black thoughts are stagnant, yet never sleep.

Encaged in night, the shadow doesn't weep,
Knowing its darkness is its greatest worth,
When the worm comes out to creep.

The shadow needs to leave the cave to seep
Into the dreamed-of terrors of my hidden heart.
Black thoughts are stagnant, yet never sleep
When the worm comes out to creep.

Black Roses

Black roses survive in soil that's not rich;
They know better than to wait for a rain's wash
Or to expect a soul to care or be within reach.
So, their petals accept their darkness without a wish.

Perhaps this is why black roses have a hoarse voice,
Which I've heard and understood best in their oath
That the black roses rasp at me as their only advice:
Live with dry dirt, absent sun, and no hope for growth.

The Desk

Now that you're gone, I'm sitting alone at your desk.
An uncoiled, bent paperclip mimics drunken lines
Weaving wildly on a twisting road, crossing lanes,
Like your Pontiac swerving that autumn day at dusk.
In a glass, beside the empty vodka bottle, a pen
Stands with its end chewed on, gnawed away,
Recalling your teeth, your lips, while the word *Why*
Repeats. A framed photo of your mouth half open

Leans beside your old calendar that marks the day
Last year when, in that crash, my life became less.
The skull shrinks, you insisted, *and then you die.*
But what words can ever explain or diminish loss?
You couldn't sustain your stoned-speed through
All those twisted and uncertain curves calling you.

The Uncertainty of Flight

He paces, describing the wax and feathers,
The fluttering effort to climb and ascend—
"The plan's perfect, Icarus," my father's
Low voice declares. I don't make a sound.

What can I say? I'm not sure what I believe;
Stuck on this hate-ridden island of Crete,
I get it. I understand the impulse to leave
By whatever means my father can create.

Even now, as the warm light blazes red
And my father's plan strikes me as decent,
I recall a dream I didn't know how to read
In which I saw a boy in a rapid descent.

I can still see that boy falling from the sky,
His legs splashing into water after miles
Of flight, and that kid, shouting, *Screw
It all*, is me, failing as my father smiles.

Squinting Below Electric Stars

Knowing full well I've lost it, I light
Out on the open road, longing to burn
In a bright town, shutting out the night.

Arriving under the electric stars of Vegas, born
For gamblers, lovers of risk, all who must prowl
An elusive score on a strip that glitters like scorn,

I know I'm meant to be here. Despite a dog's growl,
This city, where the lights glare on the unknown,
Draws in human strays who roll the dice and howl.

And, of course, I'm one of them, without a home,
Accepting that life's played out in a casino as I sit
Fondling cards and listening to fluorescents hum.

All is illuminated; all hinges on chance. Yet my sight
Is tested here, as I squint, trying to see what's changed:
I know darkness so well, but am a stranger to light.

Gambling with Madness

With Madness at my side, my escort,
Whose mere glance opens every door,
I'm led to a table where she'll hold court
If I can muster the courage to face her dare.
She challenges me not to reveal any alarm,
But blend obliquely into the casino's room,
Study my cards. Despite her lunatic charm,
I must avoid alerting *those* who threaten ruin.
Just who *they* are, she insists, never matters.
Yet I try not to listen—just gamble and hum.
I must learn to ignore when Madness mutters:
"Remember, *they* mean to do you harm."
      But I see the dealer, see the cowboy who raises my bet,
      See *them* all, and see Madness knowing I'm already beat.

At Sea in Vegas

I must've looked like a floundering fish—
Unable to stop drinking, unable to understand
The current of the cards resisting my wish
That I held a better hand, wasn't so stoned,

Wasn't sinking fast. But I was fighting a tide
Of rising bets, compelled to bluff and blink.
And though I was drawn to the bottom, I tried
To hold fast at the table and keep my face blank.

Yet not only cards and waves can be unstable.
I saw myself drowning as I heard the dealer say,
Easy does it, buddy. But washed up at the table,
Tears on my cheeks, I tasted the sea's salt spray.

Confused Proximity

Having left the casino sweating, on the strip
I park myself on a bench. Beside me, as if sent
By the gods, a young woman then sits. My grip
On all else flies beside her short skirt, her scent.
Why would such long fishnet legs spread for me
Though, an unstable loser, a fool who wants her
But won't dare turn to face her in the neon I see
As a blinding blizzard of light in harshest winter?
And how might I speak to her when my lips
Can't move? I'm a mess, shivering as hope dies.
Gusts strike my back like lashes from whips.
Does she feel it too? I'd be less alone if she does.
    "Wanna good time?" she asks. "Just three hundred dollars."
    I still can't speak, but I nod. "I'm yours then. I'm Dolores."

Cannibal Passion

When I get Dolores back to my room,

I sweep my fingers through her black hair.

Her false lashes mechanically flutter by the hour.

All of her is for hire, I think, as my hands roam;

This is what I need, a woman next to me with eyes—

Despite knowing their depths hold untold lies.

I just need someone beside me offering sighs

Into my ear, almost sounding uncontrived.

It's not that I long for painted lips pressed to mine,

As much as I need my teeth nibbling moist

Skin to satisfy my hunger to feed on the most

Willing delight I might degrade, but never define.

    Now, rolling her on her back, exposing her breasts,

    I open my mouth, baring my teeth to dine on her flesh.

Wandering on the Vegas Strip

Leaving my room, the casino, hitting the street,

Staggering by strip clubs, churches—hustlers let

Me pass, sweating for the truth of shadows, lit

By too many signs illuminating this city of defeat.

Behind an Elvis impersonator, my dead brother

Steps out now and puts a cold hand on my shoulder,

Whispering, "No drama, please." As I shudder,

He continues, "Accept the white light; don't bother

To fight its call. From the red on your hands I see

Promise—don't pretend you don't know what I mean."

I've missed my brother, loved him, but he is the man

Who deserted me. I look at him; uncertain what to say.

What's Seen and Unseen

I am well acquainted with my bloodshot eyes,
Even as they sit in their sockets and wildly stare
Up above, straining, squinting through neon skies—
I know I might as well be living on a distant star.

But my eyes' work keeps me busy. I am a machine,
Blinking, that won't break down until blind or dead.
It seems, I'll forever question what's seen and unseen.
Should my eyes and acts be refined in focus and deed

By my dark, deceased brother—knowing he's blind?
Death took his sight. But me, I can't trust my mind.

Leaving Las Vegas

Alone, under a desert sun, I leave lost Vegas,
As my brother's ghost still whispers in dust.
It seems, he found his die and tossed it, vaguely
Wishing for a winning throw, which was dashed.

As I gun the engine, I hear him: *you are free as I;*
You need no destinations, no answers to why.

Medium of Exchange

I am lonely for images with dimension
That stretch out a sky that's never enough,
When metaphor was richer and the attention
To bards, flying like birds, made us look up.

Before money became the ultimate precious
Value, the moon's silver, the sun's gold in a chant
Brought to a page something not as specious
As the contents and size of one's bank account.

Today the moon spins, but rarely gets a mention
In the *Wall Street Journal* as stocks rise and sink.
Hell, this new century tests even my own attention,
Even as I scribble these lines, look up and drink.

The Leaf

Glorious the moment was as I inhaled her scent.
But now, I'm alone in another city, in this place,
Rereading her words in the old emails she sent.
Here, her voice is not heard to quicken my pulse.
Here, there's mostly darkness, the light is scant.

The last time we were together, I noticed a leaf
Falling without a sound, without a scream of pain,
Till it hit the ground, where she stepped on it. Love,
She carelessly trampled, not hesitating to postpone—
The death of a leaf, death of us—her turning to leave.

City Nocturne Pantoum

It's always dark on my side of town:
Shadows have a franchise here.
Every alley ends up blind, just
Off the boulevard of boarded-up dreams.

Shadows have a franchise here,
Contractually bound by this controlling clause:
Off the boulevard of boarded-up dreams,
The sun is barred from showing its face.

Contractually bound by this controlling clause:
Night is the norm for my neighborhood;
The sun is barred from showing its face.
Here, all light must be snuffed out.

Night is the norm for my neighborhood:
I am never allowed to see daylight.
Here, all light must be snuffed out.
It's always dark on my side of town.

Urban Pastoral

The woods of Arcady are dead . . .
W.B. Yeats, 1889

The pastoral, forest and fields, is passé.

In the city, I cower in dark gray concrete

Shade, as my feet scuff pavement to create

A mark, shuffling midst a subway's passing

Roar. Without you, I tremble as hidden steel

Shakes dirt and rust below, and ashen faces

Above, stare down, move with clenched fists

On the sidewalk, like they're eager to steal

My soul. Spirits of the streets (not of trees,

Streams, or rocks), would have me lose my

Memories of you, our time together—sigh

For the old, faded canvas of autumn leaves.

Yet, as rats scurry by electric rails and none

Blink, I still recall you in the flickering neon.

An Easy Breath

Right now, I can't recall reciting a psalm

In a place or time where I didn't struggle

(As if throat squeezed) for an easy breath.

Yet, if suffocation does cause my death,

It'll be my wretched memories that strangle

Me, leaving me unable to ever feel calm.

On the Inheritance of Guilt

*I the LORD thy God . . . [will] visit the iniquity of the
fathers upon the children unto the third and fourth
[generation]*

--Deuteronomy 5:9

GrandEd's head was smooth and bald;

He was a man in Mussolini's mold.

Speaking chin first, with his strong jaw,

He'd pour out his vitriol when he explained

The Depression as a cabal led by The Jew

And then list the others he also blamed.

Hate-sick in his worn chair, in cigarette haze,

South of the Mason-Dixon line, his

Job as barely intact as his Maryland home,

He'd bounce me on his knee and I'd waver

Between naïve love and the sense of him

As a nightrider, brandishing a saber.

After GrandEd read news of a lynching,

He tore into his T-bone while lunching.

But today, he is long gone, and so I can't

Debate his ghost. It's impossible to choose

Now to change my silence when he'd rant

With his seething anger, his redneck blues.

Breakdown

As a boy, I heard and watched how GrandEd's

Memories, gradually embedded with grit,

Darkened, like irritated skin, in his bed's

Wrinkled sheets, as he surrendered to the great

Feast of decay, preceding complete collapse.

I saw the map across his forehead of cracks.

But, most of all, what stopped me in my tracks,

Was his foggy look when he couldn't relax

And his eyes glazed over, like he was spent,

But still wanting to understand what it all meant.

Final Words

In the end, GrandEd accepted the fog as nothing new
When he fell into full-blown dementia—without a clue—
The day, year, just who was who, he didn't know.
Memories spun on a wheel, malleable as wet clay.
When we thought he was dead, my GrandEd woke
And then spoke in throaty whispers from his bed,
Telling death to get lost and, despite being so weak,
Invoked images shifting shapes, sculpting in his head:
Ladies draped in silk dresses and gentlemen in spats,
Drivers with top hats directing carriages horse-drawn
On cobblestone—pausing only for his coughs and spits.
But his final words recalled dreams down the drain:

> "This world's a place where all's goddamn hard;
>
> Maybe the next one's easier, or so I've heard."

The Dark Hood

For Peter Roberts (1949-1987)

After GrandEd was buried, my brother's head
Bent toward the ground, fresh soil—muttered curse,
Concealing his face—when he walked to the hearse,
Trying to hide all inside, as if he wore a dark hood.
My parents, resistant to others seeing us as we were,
Would approve an abstract hood to shield one's heart—
To them, a figurative hood was *de rigueur* to avoid hurt
As creatures created from common dirt, bent to war.
I knew finely drawn cracks lined my brother's face,
Knew his tired, bloodshot blue eyes squint and gaze,
Saw him bite his lower lip, stumble, trapped in a maze,
Though all was concealed when his hood was in place.
But one winter, he tore off his hood, his disguise,
In disgust, found his face and then his own demise.

The Spark

After Peter was gone, her words bled on a pin
When mother spoke and sipped her scotch, neat.
My father failed to fathom her and Peter's pain
As my parents sat together with a drink at night.

My father's distance could cut against the grain
Of her grief and her heart's secret self. A busy job,
The stress, all my father spoke of, seemed a game
To hide my mother's spark till her head throbbed.

She knew he loved her, had loved Peter, but fears
Held my mother back, aware how he could get mad.
But the genius of her spark somehow lit its own fires,
Kept her warm, not shivering, despite father's mood.

Lines for My Mother

(1920-2007)

Near the end, she filled the old chair in her room—
Eyes squinting, red swollen knees, gnarled feet,
Arthritic hands pawing the hours—as she'd fret
In the dimming light where her memories roamed.
Sometimes she spoke about GrandEd, her father,
Or she'd say, having lost Peter so young wasn't fair,
Even though she understood life only went so far,
Even when she'd pray, each prayer, like a feather,
She knew, floated a bit, then fell down. Her voice,
Though rusted, was oiled when she spoke of plays
She wished she had staged in some public place.
Then she'd stare at flowers withering in a vase.
Today, I recall her best when she'd paint or draw
At her easel, the sun touching her hair like straw.

Words Are the Rain In My Head

I wondered, as a boy, if on earth
Rain fell everywhere but on me,
That I'd never caught a drop since birth,
Though, in the rain's scribbling I could see

Words from the sky's page. I knew rain
Had, as its raison d'être, to let life grow.
Yet, I heard most speak ill, complain
Of storms or clouds that are black or gray.

And I still see people scramble to try
Avoiding a sudden downpour, to hide.
But now, I'm glad to be soaked by the sky.
For me, words are the rain in my head.

Pursuing a Dying Art

It seems, my poems are most often bleak,
As if for me alone, where most won't see
Beneath the surface, most see only a blank.
But *so what* if, on these pages, none but me

Perceive my intent? Let others call me mad;
Say my syllables stumble, without a crutch,
Like a cripple down a ditch into the mud.
Let my words fall and fail, I know this much:

To me, it is clear what these poems mean
And, like a stalker, pursuing a dying art,
I don't have to be understood. I don't moan
To be seen. I only need to explore my heart.

Snowbound

Here is a storm at night with no end in sight.

Here is how I fall, shivering in the middle of it,

Laid flat as a slab of ice, my past, frozen in black,

Her name, I so often whispered, now just a blank.

I asked so little of her, but here I am, struck dumb,

Left numb, not picking myself up, cursing *goddamn*

To air. My breath is misting white into the snow's

Cold, like her, slapping my face. Why? God knows.

Sestets on the Cold

Mostly, I see my life passing through ice,
Where the air is pale white and cold.
I might as well be an icicle, called
Upon, shivering, to stretch and sacrifice—
Till I'm cracking up somewhere, while
She's off, making small talk with a smile.

Of course, like ice, I could easily shatter.
I must move—but can't. Instead, I'll break
Apart anytime now, I know, in a bleak
Crash, like broken glass with a shudder.
Then, aware I never had her heart deep
Or close enough to mine—I'll weep.

The Moon's an Angry Woman

I see the moon's an angry woman tonight—
Darkness deepens her eyes, even cloaked
In sable clouds. On my back, staring up, a knot
Freezing in my chest, something's clicked—

Above the snow, she broods, twists her face,
Waiting for my frozen blood to melt and spill,
Waiting for another mere mortal sacrifice,
Paralyzed, gasping for breath under her spell.

Even freezing in this field, I feel a torrent
Of silver tears—To my past, I've been a slave.
Chained to memories, enduring my torment,
I am now simply a slab, waiting for the grave.

How What's Blank Might Contain
What's Bleak

Knowing what I write is never truly mine,
I'm inclined to find myself frozen by a blank
Page lately. Maybe whiteness is its own line?
Perhaps, sans ink, paper, before I can blink,
Is perfect and has made up its own mind?

Can I trust my verses—my brain, a brittle branch
Ready to snap—on what seemed real in that snow
Last winter? I scribbled thoughts—an avalanche
Of freezing lines—but a pristine page may show
Best my blizzard in blankness by naked chance.

Revision—A Pantoum

Perhaps the final word doesn't exist;

Each line written can be written again.

Rewriting never ends; it persists,

Begs in blurred thoughts for endless revision.

Each line written can be written again:

The dirge of growing old strikes a chord—

Begs in blurred thoughts for endless revision,

If our mortality is to be clearly explored.

The dirge of growing old strikes a chord—

One needs stronger syllables to find a song

If our mortality is to be clearly explored.

Perhaps the word *dirge* is all wrong.

One needs stronger syllables to find a song

If one wishes to be clear and persist.

Perhaps the word *dirge* is all wrong.

Perhaps the final word doesn't exist.

Outrunning the Rain

Tonight, I'm up when the rain goes wild,
So I draw the heavy curtains closed
And snicker at how I'd pray as a child
When the rain was the tears of a kind God
Spilling off the cheeks of clouds for my sins.
Later, as a boy, I'd shudder, regarding rain
As only a deaf God's pitter-patter sounds,
Which frayed my nerves with a tangled pain.
And later still, as a young man, I'd race
From the sky's thunder, its sarcastic applause
For the rain—God's spit on all he can replace,
All of us who keep dying without pause.
But now, old, my heart limps toward ruin,
          And I no longer try to outrun His rain.

Desert Queen

Ahava, I long for you, even though I'm just a man,
Uncertain if I dare turn my eyes to you and look.
For you, is a glance rape? But you, ruling the sand,
Should understand—I know how you live with lack

And loss, know you feel to rule means to be shut in,
To string shadows alone over silk like a lyre,
To endure solitude in a nomad's tent and begin
Each day regarding through curtains your empire.

I simply wish you knew, I'm here, waiting through
The howling and scraping of storm-blown sand,
Till you call, speak to me, and your words throw
Law and light through every fiber of this man.

Dead Sea Questions

Ahava, can one find answers or balance
In dust, cactus, or chalky pebbled sand?
Or do answers float in waves with no sound,
Just a salty taste, inviting one into a trance?

I want to ask if there's another man: if he
Knows you like I do or satisfies your lust
As I long to? Or is there no one you trust,
Leaving us both alone by the Dead Sea?

Here, we see at the lowest point on earth,
Unable to submerge deeper, the wound
Of beauty is painful as questions that ruin
Our minds, with no answers of any worth.

A Letter to Robert Browning

Dear Robert,

I need to ask if, when you were writing, could you attest
To the contractions you endured as your verses were born?
When you delivered Old Verona to the page (a process
So few know), could you see your lines breathe and burn

Into posterity? Sordello said words could simply stretch
And fall finished from air, but I think you knew the truth.
You searched all your words to render the ultimate sketch,
Knowing a poet must be a mother, an artist, and a sleuth.

Today, there's a New York Society that admires your
Verse in Gramercy Park. Does it amuse you as we comb
Through your work, hazard a remark, or sadden you more
That so few hold the key to open the door of a poem?

It would drive me mad—but perhaps this letter's just me,
Already nuts, knowing my poems offer less than straw
Blown across a page. Unlike you, Robert, it's easy to see
My persona mangled in my work, exposed as I am, raw.

> Burn this letter,
> Tobias

Classic Ghosts

Years ago the Classic poets had flesh and bone—
Existing beyond some image of a floating, faded sheet,
Or remaining embalmed in books before I was born,
Before rap music dared to blare the most lucrative shit.

True, Sophocles is not an action hero in a video game,
Nor is Aeschylus or Euripides, yet their works' breadth
Still offers more insights for our lives than the goddamn
Digital graphics modern games show with shallow depth.

Modern eyes avoid the spectral gaze of Classic ghosts,
Not seen on Reality TV, but their works are alive, pure.
I shake my head—praise of Classics isn't heard from most,
But I know their work, not the tripe of today, will endure.

In the Ocean of Speech

Flood my sight with the letters' light.

Let Voice crash waves, and keep its pace.

Verses, like arms, will spread open, left

Open wide on deck for the page's embrace.

Wind belly canvas, nerves in the rigging,

Straining to see what seems beyond reach,

As metered feet struggle to climb, gripping

To journey toward Joy in the ocean of speech.

Here, I, sailing in the depths of the page

(Despite Joy not shown on any charts, gone

from every map—in surging fear and rage),

Can try navigate toward Joy in letters again.

      And though I throw out draft after draft,

      I still journey for Joy, steering my craft.

Another Poem about the Sea

The sea is dark; above, a hint of gray moon:
The set for a tragic play with a mediocre plot
That hardly makes sense, but offers an oration
About how my life without you is a boring plight.

At this stage, I don't need to listen to the rough
Water's pounding metronome of waves to hear
The banal oration I know is true. It's tough stuff,
Time to go or drown in my damn sadness here.

The Formality of the Page

Do I contradict myself?
Very well then I contradict myself. . .
--Walt Whitman, 1855

Sometimes I wonder why white paper

Can appear complete as is or so proper,

Stiff as a starched white shirt at church

Or in a casket? The formal touch

Of white sometimes leaves me cold.

Why must I persist at a page as if called

To strip an age with black ink over death?

Blank or coupled lines might mimic breath

Sometimes. Steady stamping metered feet

Might march language on a field to fight,

I think. So I scribble on, bent at my oak desk,

Trying, while outside, the sky yields to dusk.

    Even as, inside, a bulb replaces the sun,

    My pen will still scratch on, never done.

CODA

The Endless Fall

The question is not to remain logical. The question is to slip through and, above all—yes, above all, the question is to elude judgment. I'm not saying to avoid punishment, for punishment without judgment is bearable. It has a name, besides, that guarantees our innocence: it is called misfortune. No, on the contrary, it's a matter of dodging judgment, of avoiding being forever judged without ever having a sentence pronounced.

--Albert Camus (*The Fall*, 1956)

1.

The Descent

I descend on air down to darkness

With a soft whistle of wind breezing

Around my arms, my neck, my face

And am slowly losing touch with feeling,

Save that I'm going down, that much I understand.

There's an updraft from below, a persistent streaming.

But in this blackness there's no sky, no land,

No stars with pearl brocades gleaming.

Call it the death that leaves one awake.

Call it Hell if that's what's true.

No one is here with whom I can speak;

Nothing is here to be old or new.

Perhaps this is what gets left between to be

And not to be, more limbo where I cannot see.

2.

Into the Pitch

There—I hear it, within this darkness,

A faint whispering sound not far from me.

Might there be words in this place—

Syllables so near, but I can't see

Or hear right. And when I try

To speak, no words come out of my mouth.

Sound, but not speech. The word, "why,"

Is stuck in my throat. Is *an other* a myth?

No, no, there has to be another—

An other also descending into the pitch.

But, if I lack sight or speech,

How can I know if I have or ever had a brother

Or a lover? And now, alone—where is peace

In the darkness which saturates this place?

3.

Mute Darkness

Falling through air, through black gauze,
I now glimpse a hint of light, a dim speck.
But as it's nowhere near, and I can't pause
In my descent, I won't struggle to speak
Or call to the light, though I long to rant,
Curse—what can I say? Light scratches black
Ineffectively, leaving me in the dark, ignorant.
What do I know, as I roll on my back,
Wondering if *an other* shares this night?
Might an eye be observing me out there,
Might it mean this endless fall isn't for naught?
The speck of light seems to say, "I am here,"
But the darkness is otherwise mute,
Same as a man without a brother or a mate.

Tobias Roberts was born in Rome, Italy in 1953. After returning to America for college, he graduated with a BA in History and Latin from Dickinson College and received a Masters in Classics in 1980. He taught Latin and History at Ohio State University until he decided to retire from academia and devote all his attention to his writing. *The Formality of the Page* is his first collection of poems. He currently lives in Portland, Oregon.

MICHAL AJVAZ, *The Golden Age.*
The Other City.
PIERRE ALBERT-BIROT, *Grabinoulor.*
YUZ ALESHKOVSKY, *Kangaroo.*
SVETLANA ALEXIEVICH, *Voices from Chernobyl.*
FELIPE ALFAU, *Chromos.*
Locos.
JOAO ALMINO, *Enigmas of Spring.*
IVAN ÂNGELO, *The Celebration.*
The Tower of Glass.
ANTÓNIO LOBO ANTUNES, *Knowledge of Hell.*
The Splendor of Portugal.
ALAIN ARIAS-MISSON, *Theatre of Incest.*
JOHN ASHBERY & JAMES SCHUYLER, *A Nest of Ninnies.*
GABRIELA AVIGUR-ROTEM, *Heatwave and Crazy Birds.*
DJUNA BARNES, *Ladies Almanack.*
Ryder.
JOHN BARTH, *Letters.*
Sabbatical.
Collected Stories.
DONALD BARTHELME, *The King.*
Paradise.
SVETISLAV BASARA, *Chinese Letter.*
Fata Morgana.
In Search of the Grail.
MIQUEL BAUÇÀ, *The Siege in the Room.*
RENÉ BELLETTO, *Dying.*
MAREK BIENCZYK, *Transparency.*
ANDREI BITOV, *Pushkin House.*
ANDREJ BLATNIK, *You Do Understand.*
Law of Desire.
LOUIS PAUL BOON, *Chapel Road.*
My Little War.
Summer in Termuren.
ROGER BOYLAN, *Killoyle.*
IGNÁCIO DE LOYOLA BRANDÃO, *Anonymous Celebrity.*
Zero.
BRIGID BROPHY, *In Transit.*
The Prancing Novelist.

GABRIELLE BURTON, *Heartbreak Hotel.*
MICHEL BUTOR, *Degrees.*
Mobile.
G. CABRERA INFANTE, *Infante's Inferno.*
Three Trapped Tigers.
JULIETA CAMPOS, *The Fear of Losing Eurydice.*
ANNE CARSON, *Eros the Bittersweet.*
ORLY CASTEL-BLOOM, *Dolly City.*
LOUIS-FERDINAND CÉLINE, *North.*
Conversations with Professor Y.
London Bridge.
HUGO CHARTERIS, *The Tide Is Right.*
ERIC CHEVILLARD, *Demolishing Nisard.*
The Author and Me.
MARC CHOLODENKO, *Mordechai Schamz.*
EMILY HOLMES COLEMAN, *The Shutter of Snow.*
ERIC CHEVILLARD, *The Author and Me.*
LUIS CHITARRONI, *The No Variations.*
CH'OE YUN, *Mannequin.*
ROBERT COOVER, *A Night at the Movies.*
STANLEY CRAWFORD, *Log of the S.S. The Mrs Unguentine.*
Some Instructions to My Wife.
RALPH CUSACK, *Cadenza.*
NICHOLAS DELBANCO, *Sherbrookes.*
The Count of Concord.
NIGEL DENNIS, *Cards of Identity.*
PETER DIMOCK, *A Short Rhetoric for Leaving the Family.*
ARIEL DORFMAN, *Konfidenz.*
COLEMAN DOWELL, *Island People.*
Too Much Flesh and Jabez.
RIKKI DUCORNET, *Phosphor in Dreamland.*
The Complete Butcher's Tales.
RIKKI DUCORNET (cont.), *The Jade Cabinet.*
The Fountains of Neptune.
WILLIAM EASTLAKE, *Castle Keep.*
Lyric of the Circle Heart.
JEAN ECHENOZ, *Chopin's Move.*

STANLEY ELKIN, *A Bad Man.*
The Dick Gibson Show.
The Franchiser.

FRANÇOIS EMMANUEL, *Invitation to a Voyage.*

SALVADOR ESPRIU, *Ariadne in the Grotesque Labyrinth.*

LESLIE A. FIEDLER, *Love and Death in the American Novel.*

JUAN FILLOY, *Op Oloop.*

GUSTAVE FLAUBERT, *Bouvard and Pécuchet.*

JON FOSSE, *Aliss at the Fire.*
Melancholy.
Trilogy.

FORD MADOX FORD, *The March of Literature.*

MAX FRISCH, *I'm Not Stiller.*
Man in the Holocene.

CARLOS FUENTES, *Christopher Unborn.*
Distant Relations.
Terra Nostra.
Where the Air Is Clear.
Nietzsche on His Balcony.

WILLIAM GADDIS, JR., *The Recognitions.*
JR.

JANICE GALLOWAY, *Foreign Parts.*
The Trick Is to Keep Breathing.

WILLIAM H. GASS, *Life Sentences.*
The Tunnel.
The World Within the Word.
Willie Masters' Lonesome Wife.

GÉRARD GAVARRY, *Hoppla! 1 2 3.*

ETIENNE GILSON, *The Arts of the Beautiful.*
Forms and Substances in the Arts.

C. S. GISCOMBE, *Giscome Road.*
Here.

DOUGLAS GLOVER, *Bad News of the Heart.*

WITOLD GOMBROWICZ, *A Kind of Testament.*

PAULO EMÍLIO SALES GOMES, *P's Three Women.*

GEORGI GOSPODINOV, *Natural Novel.*

JUAN GOYTISOLO, *Juan the Landless.*
Makbara.
Marks of Identity.

JACK GREEN, *Fire the Bastards!*

JIŘÍ GRUŠA, *The Questionnaire.*

MELA HARTWIG, *Am I a Redundant Human Being?*

JOHN HAWKES, *The Passion Artist.*
Whistlejacket.

ELIZABETH HEIGHWAY, ED., *Contemporary Georgian Fiction.*

AIDAN HIGGINS, *Balcony of Europe.*
Blind Man's Bluff.
Bornholm Night-Ferry.
Langrishe, Go Down.
Scenes from a Receding Past.

ALDOUS HUXLEY, *Antic Hay.*
Point Counter Point.
Those Barren Leaves.
Time Must Have a Stop.

JANG JUNG-IL, *When Adam Opens His Eyes*

DRAGO JANČAR, *The Tree with No Name.*
I Saw Her That Night.
Galley Slave.

MIKHEIL JAVAKHISHVILI, *Kvachi.*

GERT JONKE, *The Distant Sound.*
Homage to Czerny.
The System of Vienna.

JACQUES JOUET, *Mountain R.*
Savage.
Upstaged.

JUNG YOUNG-MOON, *A Contrived World.*

MIEKO KANAI, *The Word Book.*

YORAM KANIUK, *Life on Sandpaper.*

ZURAB KARUMIDZE, *Dagny.*

PABLO KATCHADJIAN, *What to Do.*

JOHN KELLY, *From Out of the City.*

HUGH KENNER, *Flaubert, Joyce and Beckett: The Stoic Comedians.*
Joyce's Voices.

DANILO KIŠ, *The Attic.*
The Lute and the Scars.
Psalm 44.
A Tomb for Boris Davidovich.

ANITA KONKKA, *A Fool's Paradise.*

GEORGE KONRÁD, *The City Builder.*

TADEUSZ KONWICKI, *A Minor Apocalypse.*

The Polish Complex.

ELAINE KRAF, *The Princess of 72nd Street.*

JIM KRUSOE, *Iceland.*

AYSE KULIN, *Farewell: A Mansion in Occupied Istanbul.*

EMILIO LASCANO TEGUI, *On Elegance While Sleeping.*

ERIC LAURRENT, *Do Not Touch.*

VIOLETTE LEDUC, *La Bâtarde.*

LEE KI-HO, *At Least We Can Apologize.*

EDOUARD LEVÉ, *Autoportrait.*

Suicide.

MARIO LEVI, *Istanbul Was a Fairy Tale.*

DEBORAH LEVY, *Billy and Girl.*

JOSÉ LEZAMA LIMA, *Paradiso.*

OSMAN LINS, *Avalovara.*

The Queen of the Prisons of Greece.

ALF MACLOCHLAINN, *Out of Focus.*

Past Habitual.

RON LOEWINSOHN, *Magnetic Field(s).*

YURI LOTMAN, *Non-Memoirs.*

D. KEITH MANO, *Take Five.*

MINA LOY, *Stories and Essays of Mina Loy.*

MICHELINE AHARONIAN MARCOM, *The Mirror in the Well.*

BEN MARCUS, *The Age of Wire and String.*

WALLACE MARKFIELD, *Teitlebaum's Window.*

To an Early Grave.

DAVID MARKSON, *Reader's Block.*

Wittgenstein's Mistress.

CAROLE MASO, *AVA.*

HISAKI MATSUURA, *Triangle.*

LADISLAV MATEJKA & KRYSTYNA POMORSKA, EDS., *Readings in Russian Poetics: Formalist & Structuralist Views.*

HARRY MATHEWS, *Cigarettes.*

The Conversions.

The Human Country.

The Journalist.

My Life in CIA.

Singular Pleasures.

The Sinking of the Odradek.

Stadium.

Tlooth.

JOSEPH MCELROY, *Night Soul and Other Stories.*

ABDELWAHAB MEDDEB, *Talismano.*

GERHARD MEIER, *Isle of the Dead.*

HERMAN MELVILLE, *The Confidence-Man.*

AMANDA MICHALOPOULOU, *I'd Like.*

STEVEN MILLHAUSER, *The Barnum Museum.*

In the Penny Arcade.

RALPH J. MILLS, JR., *Essays on Poetry.*

CHRISTINE MONTALBETTI, *The Origin of Man.*

Western.

NICHOLAS MOSLEY, *Accident.*

Assassins.

Catastrophe Practice.

Hopeful Monsters.

Imago Bird.

Natalie Natalia.

Serpent.

WARREN MOTTE, *Fiction Now: The French Novel in the 21st Century.*

Oulipo: A Primer of Potential Literature.

GERALD MURNANE, *Barley Patch.*

Inland.

YVES NAVARRE, *Our Share of Time.*

Sweet Tooth.

DOROTHY NELSON, *In Night's City.*

Tar and Feathers.

WILFRIDO D. NOLLEDO, *But for the Lovers.*

BORIS A. NOVAK, *The Master of Insomnia.*

FLANN O'BRIEN, *At Swim-Two-Birds.*

The Best of Myles.

The Dalkey Archive.

The Hard Life.

The Poor Mouth.

The Third Policeman.

CLAUDE OLLIER, *The Mise-en-Scène.*

Wert and the Life Without End.

PATRIK OUŘEDNÍK, *Europeana.*
The Opportune Moment, 1855.

BORIS PAHOR, *Necropolis.*

FERNANDO DEL PASO, *News from the Empire.*
Palinuro of Mexico.

ROBERT PINGET, *The Inquisitory.*
Mahu or The Material.
Trio.

MANUEL PUIG, *Betrayed by Rita Hayworth.*
The Buenos Aires Affair.
Heartbreak Tango.

RAYMOND QUENEAU, *The Last Days.*
Odile.
Pierrot Mon Ami.
Saint Glinglin.

ANN QUIN, *Berg.*
Passages.
Three.
Tripticks.

ISHMAEL REED, *The Free-Lance Pallbearers.*
The Last Days of Louisiana Red.
Ishmael Reed: The Plays.
Juice!
The Terrible Threes.
The Terrible Twos.
Yellow Back Radio Broke-Down.

RAINER MARIA RILKE,
The Notebooks of Malte Laurids Brigge.

JULIÁN RÍOS, *The House of Ulysses.*
Larva: A Midsummer Night's Babel.
Poundemonium.

ALAIN ROBBE-GRILLET, *Project for a Revolution in New York.*
A Sentimental Novel.

AUGUSTO ROA BASTOS, *I the Supreme.*

DANIËL ROBBERECHTS, *Arriving in Avignon.*

JEAN ROLIN, *The Explosion of the Radiator Hose.*

OLIVIER ROLIN, *Hotel Crystal.*

ALIX CLEO ROUBAUD, *Alix's Journal.*

JACQUES ROUBAUD, *The Form of a City Changes Faster, Alas, Than the Human Heart.*

The Great Fire of London.
Hortense in Exile.
Hortense Is Abducted.
Mathematics: The Plurality of Worlds of Lewis.
Some Thing Black.

RAYMOND ROUSSEL, *Impressions of Africa.*

VEDRANA RUDAN, *Night.*

GERMAN SADULAEV, *The Maya Pill.*

TOMAŽ ŠALAMUN, *Soy Realidad.*

LYDIE SALVAYRE, *The Company of Ghosts.*

LUIS RAFAEL SÁNCHEZ, *Macho Camacho's Beat.*

SEVERO SARDUY, *Cobra & Maitreya.*

NATHALIE SARRAUTE, *Do You Hear Them?*
Martereau.
The Planetarium.

STIG SÆTERBAKKEN, *Siamese.*
Self-Control.
Through the Night.

ARNO SCHMIDT, *Collected Novellas.*
Collected Stories.
Nobodaddy's Children.
Two Novels.

ASAF SCHURR, *Motti.*

GAIL SCOTT, *My Paris.*

JUNE AKERS SEESE,
Is This What Other Women Feel Too?

BERNARD SHARE, *Inish.*
Transit.

VIKTOR SHKLOVSKY, *Bowstring.*
Literature and Cinematography.
Theory of Prose.
Third Factory.
Zoo, or Letters Not about Love.

PIERRE SINIAC, *The Collaborators.*

KJERSTI A. SKOMSVOLD,
The Faster I Walk, the Smaller I Am.

JOSEF ŠKVORECKÝ, *The Engineer of Human Souls.*

GILBERT SORRENTINO, *Aberration of Starlight.*
Blue Pastoral.
Crystal Vision.

Imaginative Qualities of Actual Things.
Mulligan Stew.
Red the Fiend.
Steelwork.
Under the Shadow.
ANDRZEJ STASIUK, *Dukla.*
Fado.
GERTRUDE STEIN, *The Making of Americans.*
A Novel of Thank You.
PIOTR SZEWC, *Annihilation.*
GONÇALO M. TAVARES, *A Man: Klaus Klump.*
Jerusalem.
Learning to Pray in the Age of Technique.
LUCIAN DAN TEODOROVICI, *Our Circus Presents...*
NIKANOR TERATOLOGEN, *Assisted Living.*
STEFAN THEMERSON, *Hobson's Island.*
The Mystery of the Sardine.
Tom Harris.
JOHN TOOMEY, *Sleepwalker.*
Huddleston Road.
Slipping.
DUMITRU TSEPENEAG, *Hotel Europa.*
The Necessary Marriage.
Pigeon Post.
Vain Art of the Fugue.
La Belle Roumaine.
Waiting: Stories.
ESTHER TUSQUETS, *Stranded.*
DUBRAVKA UGRESIC, *Lend Me Your Character.*
Thank You for Not Reading.
TOR ULVEN, *Replacement.*
MATI UNT, *Brecht at Night.*
Diary of a Blood Donor.
Things in the Night.
ÁLVARO URIBE & OLIVIA SEARS, EDS., *Best of Contemporary Mexican Fiction.*
ELOY URROZ, *Friction.*
The Obstacles.
LUISA VALENZUELA, *Dark Desires and the Others.*
He Who Searches.

PAUL VERHAEGHEN, *Omega Minor.*
BORIS VIAN, *Heartsnatcher.*
TOOMAS VINT, *An Unending Landscape.*
ORNELA VORPSI, *The Country Where No One Ever Dies.*
AUSTRYN WAINHOUSE, *Hedyphagetica.*
MARKUS WERNER, *Cold Shoulder.*
Zundel's Exit.
CURTIS WHITE, *The Idea of Home.*
Memories of My Father Watching TV.
Requiem.
DIANE WILLIAMS, *Excitability: Selected Stories.*
DOUGLAS WOOLF, *Wall to Wall.*
Ya! & John-Juan.
JAY WRIGHT, *Polynomials and Pollen.*
The Presentable Art of Reading Absence.
PHILIP WYLIE, *Generation of Vipers.*
MARGUERITE YOUNG, *Angel in the Forest.*
Miss MacIntosh, My Darling.
REYOUNG, *Unbabbling.*
ZORAN ŽIVKOVIĆ , *Hidden Camera.*
LOUIS ZUKOFSKY, *Collected Fiction.*
VITOMIL ZUPAN, *Minuet for Guitar.*
SCOTT ZWIREN, *God Head.*

AND MORE . . .